Michelle Kwan

by Rosemary Wallner

Reading Consultant:
Dr. Robert Miller
Professor of Special Education
Minnesota State University, Mankato

CAPSTONE
HIGH-INTEREST
BOOKS

an imprint of Capstone Press
Mankato, Minnesota

Capstone High-Interest Books are published by Capstone Press
151 Good Counsel Drive, P.O. Box 669, Mankato, Minnesota 56002
http://www.capstone-press.com

Library of Congress Cataloging-in-Publication Data
Wallner, Rosemary, 1964–
    Michelle Kwan/by Rosemary Wallner.
    p. cm.—(Sports heroes)
    Includes bibliographical references and index.
    ISBN 0-7368-0779-9
    1. Kwan, Michelle, 1980—Juvenile literature. 2. Skaters—United States—
Biography—Juvenile literature. 3. Women skaters—United States—Biography—
Juvenile literature. [1. Kwan, Michelle, 1980– 2. Ice skaters. 3. Chinese Americans—
Biography. 4. Women—Biography.] I. Title. II. Series: Sports heroes (Mankato, Minn.)
GV850.K93 W35 2001
796.91'2'092—dc21   00-010092

Summary: Traces the personal life and career of the world-champion figure skater.

Editorial Credits
Angela Kaelberer and Matt Doeden, editors; Lois Wallentine, product planning editor;
    Timothy Halldin, cover designer and illustrator; Katy Kudela, photo researcher

Photo Credits
Allsport USA/Mike Powell, 13, 20; Clive Brunskill, 14; Tony Duffy, 17, 19;
    Jed Jacobsohn, 27; Jamie Squire, 32; Matthew Stockman, 34
AP/Wide World Photos/Rusty Kennedy, cover
Reuters/Barbara L. Johnson/Archive Photos, 31
Reuters/Fred Prouser/Archive Photos, 23
Reuters/Gary Hershorn/Archive Photos, 36
Reuters/Ron Schwane/Archive Photos, 42
SportsChrome-USA/Bob Tringali, 4, 9, 10, 38, 41; Mark Friedman, 7; Rob Tringali Jr.,
    24, 28

2 3 4 5 6 06 05 04 03 02 01

Table of Contents

CHAPTER 1

World Champion

It was April 1, 2000. Michelle Kwan stepped onto the ice of the Palais des Expositions arena in Nice, France. The lights shone bright. The crowd sat quietly and waited for the music to begin.

Michelle was skating in the long program in the World Figure Skating Championships. She was the first skater in the long program group to take the ice. Michelle knew that this position is not always best for a skater. The judges often give the first skater slightly lower marks than later skaters. They score this way in case another skater does very well later in the competition.

Michelle was the first skater in the long program at the 2000 World Figure Skating Championships.

Michelle was in third place after the short program. The judges had placed Russian skaters Maria Butyrskaya and Irina Slutskaya ahead of her. But the long program was 50 percent of Michelle's final score. She would win the title if she placed first in the long program.

Michelle began to skate to the music of "The Red Violin" by John Corigliano. She completed her first triple jump. It was a triple loop. She then completed a triple-double combination jump. She completed six triples during the program. One was a triple toe-triple toe combination. She had never completed a triple-triple combination in competition before.

Michelle finished her program without making any mistakes. The crowd stood and cheered. Michelle was pleased with her performance. Her scores were good. The judges gave her mainly 5.7s and 5.8s for technical merit. She earned all 5.8s and 5.9s for presentation.

Michelle's performance earned her the gold medal at the 2000 World Figure Skating Championships.

Michelle tried to calm herself as she waited in the warm-up room. Her opponents were now skating. Michelle was too nervous to watch their performances. She lay down and stretched. Michelle told herself that she had just completed one of the best programs of her life. She would be happy no matter what happened.

The final judging was in. Michelle was the 2000 world champion. She cried as she stood on the podium and accepted the gold medal.

About Michelle Kwan

Michelle Kwan is an Olympic-eligible figure skater. She skates for the U.S. Figure Skating Association (USFSA). Michelle competes in events that are approved either by the USFSA or the International Skating Union (ISU). Michelle is an Olympic silver medalist. She won the second-place medal at the 1998 Winter Olympics in Nagano, Japan.

Michelle began her skating career at age 5. She has skated in competitions throughout the world. In 1998, she was the first skater to receive eight perfect 6.0 scores at the U.S. Figure Skating Championships. She is the first U.S. woman to win three world championship titles since Peggy Fleming won her third in 1968. Michelle won her first two world championship titles in 1996 and 1998.

Michelle Kwan

Major Skating Competition Finishes

Season	Event	Place
1993–94	1994 U.S. Championships	2nd
	1994 World Championships	8th
1994–95	1995 U.S. Championships	2nd
	1995 World Championships	4th
1995–96	1996 U.S. Championships	1st
	1996 World Championships	1st
1996–97	1997 U.S. Championships	2nd
	1997 World Championships	2nd
1997–98	1998 U.S. Championships	1st
	1998 Winter Olympics	2nd
	1998 World Championships	1st
1998–99	1999 U.S. Championships	1st
	1999 World Championships	2nd
1999–2000	2000 U.S. Championships	1st
	2000 World Championships	1st
2000-2001	2001 U.S. Championships	1st
	2001 World Championships	1st

CHAPTER 2

The Early Years

Michelle Kwan was born July 7, 1980, in Torrance, California. This city is about 20 miles (32 kilometers) south of Los Angeles. Michelle's parents are Danny and Estella Kwan. Both Danny and Estella were born in China. They moved to the United States in the early 1970s. Michelle is the youngest of three children. Ron is four years older and Karen is two years older than Michelle.

Danny worked as a systems analyst for Pacific Bell Telephone Company. Estella managed the family's restaurant. The restaurant was called the Golden Pheasant.

Michelle was born July 7, 1980.

An Early Interest in Skating

Michelle first skated when she was 5 years old. Michelle and Karen watched Ron skate at hockey practice. The girls asked their parents if they could take skating lessons as well.

Michelle and Karen began to take weekly lessons. Both girls enjoyed skating and showed talent for the sport. Their teacher suggested that they take private lessons. The girls soon were taking five lessons each week.

Many of Michelle's and Karen's private lessons were in the morning before school. They had to get up at 4:30. The girls often slept in their skating outfits so they would not waste any time getting dressed.

Michelle soon wanted to compete in skating events. She entered and won her first competition when she was 7. The next year, Michelle watched the 1988 Winter Olympics on TV. Her favorite skater was U.S. skater Brian Boitano. Boitano won the men's gold medal that year. Michelle decided then that she wanted to be an Olympic champion someday.

Michelle and her sister, Karen, both are talented figure skaters.

But she did not realize how hard skaters must work to make the Olympic team. She thought that all skaters were allowed to compete in the Olympics.

Danny and Estella heard about a special training center for skaters. The center was called the Ice Castle International Training Center. It was in Lake Arrowhead, California. This city is about 100 miles (160 kilometers)

Brian Boitano

In 1988, 7-year-old Michelle watched the Winter Olympics on TV. She enjoyed many of the skaters' performances. But her favorite was U.S. skater Brian Boitano.

Like Michelle, Boitano began his skating career at a young age. In 1979, he began competing at the senior level. He was 16 at the time. In 1982, he became the first American skater to successfully perform a triple axel in competition.

Boitano won the men's title at the U.S. Championships in 1985, 1986, 1987, and 1988. He was the world champion in 1986 and 1988. In 1988, he won the Olympic gold medal. Boitano turned professional after the 1988 World Championships. He and Michelle became friends when they toured with the Tour of World Figure Skating Champions ice show. Today, Boitano still watches Michelle compete whenever he can. He also gives her advice about skating.

northeast of Torrance. The family began driving the two hours to the center on the weekends. They stayed in a friend's cabin. Michelle and Karen took lessons as often as their parents could afford them.

A Year of Changes

The Ice Castle International Skating Foundation gave scholarships to Michelle and Karen in 1990. The money from these scholarships helped the Kwans pay for the girls' lessons and skating costs. The Kwans then hired top skating coach Frank Carroll to work with Michelle and Karen.

Danny and the girls moved to Lake Arrowhead. They lived in a one-room cabin. Estella and Ron stayed in Torrance to run the restaurant. The entire family was together only on weekends.

Michelle and Karen began taking regular private lessons three days each week. A tutor helped them with their school lessons. Danny tried not to miss any practices. He watched the girls skate before school. He then drove the two hours to work. He returned to Lake Arrowhead in the evening.

Skating Costs

Michelle's and Karen's skating expenses increased even with the scholarships. The Kwans had to pay for the girls' time on the ice. As they grew, their skates needed to be replaced. They also needed new costumes for competitions. These costumes can cost as much as $1,000. Danny and Estella had to sell their house in order to pay some of these costs. In 1993, Danny estimated that he paid about $50,000 to $60,000 a year to keep the girls at the center. But he said that the money was not a sacrifice. He wanted to give his talented daughters the gift of skating.

Michelle began to train three hours each day. She also worked out in the gym for about one hour each day. Before and after skating, Michelle fit in time for school. She studied for about three hours each day with a private tutor.

In 1993, Michelle prepared for the Winter Olympics.

Moving to the Senior Level

Women's singles skating has eight levels. The lowest level is pre-preliminary and the highest is senior ladies. Skaters must pass a test to move to a higher level. Most skaters spend a year at each level. They master the necessary jumps, spins, and spirals. But Michelle quickly learned and mastered each new move. By

1992, she performed all the jumps necessary to compete at the senior level.

In January 1992, 11-year-old Michelle qualified for the U.S. Junior National Championships. But she skated poorly that day. She finished in ninth place. Michelle and Carroll were disappointed. Despite the loss, Michelle said she wanted to skate at the senior level. But Carroll thought she needed more experience. He wanted her to stay a junior until she gained more maturity and style.

In May 1992, Michelle took the senior test while Carroll was out of town. She skated in front of a panel of judges. Michelle passed the test. She was ready to compete against skaters who were five to 10 years older than she was.

Carroll was angry that Michelle had disobeyed him. But Michelle told him that she wanted to challenge herself against the best. Carroll told Michelle that they would have to work even harder than before. He did not want Michelle to embarrass herself in front of the other senior skaters. Michelle agreed. She told Carroll that her goal was to compete in the 1994 Winter Olympics.

Michelle was skating as a senior by age 12.

CHAPTER 3

Mastering the Sport

During the 1992–93 skating season, Michelle began to receive national attention. She became the youngest senior competitor at the U.S. Championships in Phoenix, Arizona. She finished sixth. In July 1993, Michelle won her first major senior title. She won the Olympic Festival in San Antonio, Texas. At that event, she landed six triple jumps in front of a crowd of about 25,000 people. She became the Olympic Festival's youngest skating champion.

At age 12, Michelle was the youngest senior competitor at the U.S. Championships.

A Growing Sport

Before 1994, sportswriters did not pay much attention to young skaters like Michelle. Most people only were interested in skaters who had won Olympic medals. That situation changed in 1994. The event that changed the sport involved two top U.S. skaters. Their names were Nancy Kerrigan and Tonya Harding.

The 1994 U.S. Championships took place in Detroit, Michigan. Kerrigan was at an ice rink after a practice session. A man suddenly came out of the stands. He hit Kerrigan's knee with a heavy club and ran away. Doctors told Kerrigan that it would take several weeks to heal the wound. Officials later proved that friends and relatives of Harding hired the man to injure Kerrigan. Stories of the crime and of the two skaters filled newspapers and magazines.

Reports of the crime increased many people's interest in figure skating. They wanted to hear about other skaters. Michelle was doing well in the competitions she

Michelle was named the first alternate to the 1994 Winter Olympics.

entered. Many newspapers, magazines, and TV shows began reporting about her.

Olympic Dreams

Harding won first place at the 1994 U.S. Championships. Michelle won second. Kerrigan sat out the event while her leg healed. The top two finishers usually are allowed on the Olympic team. But USFSA officials

Michelle updated her image for the 1995 U.S. Nationals.

decided that Kerrigan should be on the team with Harding. The officials said that Kerrigan's past record of wins earned her a place on the team. They named Michelle the first alternate. Michelle would skate in the Olympics only if Harding or Kerrigan could not compete.

Michelle took the news well. She told reporters that she was disappointed she would not be able to compete. But she added that

Kerrigan deserved the opportunity to compete in the Olympics.

A Breakout Season

After the Olympics, Michelle and her coach decided to update Michelle's image. They wanted Michelle to look more mature on the ice. Carroll talked the Kwans into letting Michelle wear makeup while she competed. He suggested that she get rid of her ponytail hairstyle. Michelle began to wear her hair up in a bun.

Carroll also helped Michelle work on her free-skating program. She began including six or seven triple jumps in her program. At the time, most female skaters' programs had four or five triples. Michelle also began to practice the difficult triple axel. This jump is difficult because skaters must rotate their bodies three-and-one-half times in the air. They must also switch their skating position from forward to backward during the jump. Few women are able to perform this jump.

It's incredible for me to have such a high achievement. It's always been my dream, ever since I was a little girl, and now ... it's true.
—Michelle Kwan, Knight-Ridder/Tribune News Service, 1/23/96

The new ideas and hard work paid off. In 1995, Michelle placed second to Nicole Bobek at the U.S. Nationals in Providence, Rhode Island. Karen also competed at the championships. She placed seventh. Later that year, Michelle placed fourth at the World Championships in Birmingham, England.

Career Changes

In 1995, Carroll and choreographer Lori Nichol developed a new long program for Michelle. Choreographers help skaters plan their jumps and spins to go with pieces of music. Michelle skated to "Salome" by Richard Strauss. Michelle skated this program to become both the 1996 U.S. and world champion. At the Worlds, the judges awarded her two perfect 6.0 scores. The 6.0s were the first of Michelle's career. At 15, she also was the youngest U.S. woman to win a world championship.

After her victories, promoter Tom Collins invited Michelle to skate in his Tour of World Figure Skating Champions ice show. She spent

Michelle won her first world championship title in 1996.

three months touring North America with other top skaters.

Michelle's body began changing as well. She grew 7 inches (18 centimeters) and gained 19 pounds (8.6 kilograms). Her height was now 5 feet, 2 inches (1.6 meters). She weighed 96 pounds (44 kilograms). Changes in height and weight often affect a skater's balance. A change in balance can affect a skater's jumps. Michelle adjusted to the changes in her body.

CHAPTER 4

The Road to the Olympics

Sixteen-year-old Michelle began the 1996–97 season as the U.S. and world champion. Many fans and skating experts believed she would become the youngest U.S. skater to win a gold medal at the 1998 Winter Olympics. Michelle made many appearances in competitions and other events. She was earning almost $1 million a year from skating tours, prize money, and endorsements.

The Olympics still were a year away. But experts already considered Michelle to be the top U.S. female figure skater. She and Carroll

Michelle began the 1996–97 season as the U.S. and world champion.

had created an even more difficult program. Michelle's new program included seven triple jumps. Three of them occurred in the final minute. Most skaters are too tired to perform difficult jumps during the last minute of their programs.

But Michelle was not as successful as she had hoped. Fourteen-year-old skater Tara Lipinski defeated Michelle in many competitions in 1997. In February 1997, Michelle faced Lipinski at the U.S. Nationals in Nashville, Tennessee. Michelle fell three times during her program. She placed second to Lipinski in the competition.

A month later, the two skaters met at the World Championships in Lausanne, Switzerland. Again, Michelle came in second place. Lipinski became the world champion.

Eye on the Olympics
Michelle knew that she had to improve her attitude about skating in order to perform better at competitions. She thought about

Michelle won first place at the 1998 U.S. Nationals.

reasons for skating. Michelle realized that she skated because she enjoyed the sport. She knew that she needed to show this enjoyment during her performances.

Michelle took her new attitude to the 1998 U.S. Nationals in Philadelphia, Pennsylvania. Seven of the nine judges awarded Michelle a 6.0 for presentation in her short program. She received eight 6.0s for presentation in her long

Michelle and Frank Carroll learned backstage that she had placed second in the Olympics.

program. No other American skater had ever received that many perfect scores at the U.S. Nationals. Michelle's victory meant she was the leader of the 1998 U.S. Olympic team. Lipinski earned the second spot on the team.

The Olympics

The 1998 Winter Olympics were held in Nagano, Japan. Throughout the Olympic competition, Michelle skated with grace and skill. She was in first place after the short program. Michelle's long program also went well. She did not receive any 6.0 scores. But her scores of 5.7s and 5.8s for technical merit and 5.9s for presentation were very good.

Lipinski skated second to last during the long program competition. Like Michelle, she skated an excellent long program. Six of the nine judges ranked her ahead of Michelle. Lipinski won the gold medal. Michelle received the silver medal.

Backstage, Michelle heard that she had placed second. She was crushed. Her friends and family members comforted her. They blamed her loss on bad judging. But Carroll knew better. He later took Michelle aside and told her that she had skated well. But it was not her greatest performance.

Michelle thought about what Carroll had said. Her attitude improved. She then began thinking about the next Olympics. She knew that she could improve her skating.

CHAPTER 5

Michelle Kwan Today

Michelle came back a winner during the rest of the 1997–98 season. Lipinski turned professional after winning the Olympic gold medal. Lipinski then could not compete at the World Championships in Minneapolis, Minnesota. Michelle skated well to win her second world championship title.

In June 1998, Michelle earned her high school diploma. She also began preparing to attend the University of California in Los Angeles (UCLA).

Michelle won her second world championship in 1998.

In August 1998, Michelle did something that she had not done in her 13 years of skating. She took a month off from training. The Kwans took their first family vacation. They went to Hawaii. Michelle went scuba diving and snorkeling.

Michelle returned to her busy schedule after her vacation. She took dance classes, lifted weights, ran, and skated. Michelle also was named Sportswoman of the Year by the Women's Sports Foundation.

Michelle won another U.S. championship title in 1999. But she placed second at the World Championships in March. She lost to Maria Butyrskaya.

Recent Events

Michelle began the fall of 1999 as a college student. She moved into a room in a UCLA dormitory. It was the first time that she had lived away from home. Michelle enjoyed her classes and making new friends.

Michelle won another U.S. championship title in 1999.

Michelle continued to compete in skating competitions during the 1999–2000 season. She did her best to balance the demands of school and training. But many skating experts thought that Michelle's busy schedule caused her skating to suffer. She fell at least once during most competitions. But she also won competitions such as Skate America and Skate Canada.

In February, Michelle competed in the U.S. Nationals. Michelle fell during both the short and long programs. But the judges enjoyed her style and gave her good scores. She won the competition.

Michelle knew that she had to skate her best to win the 2000 World Championships. She practiced a difficult triple-triple combination. Michelle had never tried this combination in competition before.

At the World Championships, Michelle again struggled with her jumps. During the short program, she wobbled on the landing of

Michelle won the 2000 U.S. Nationals.

a triple flip. That mistake brought her down to third place. But Michelle did not give up. She skated a great long program to win the championship.

In 2001, Michelle again won the U.S. Nationals. She then competed at the World Championships in Vancouver, British Columbia. At the World Championships, Michelle performed six triple jumps to win the title.

Michelle's Future

Michelle plans to continue her college education at UCLA. She plans to use her education when she retires from skating.

Michelle has one more goal to accomplish before she retires. She wants to win an Olympic gold medal. The 2002 Olympics will be held in Salt Lake City, Utah. Michelle is preparing to compete there.

Michelle wants to win a gold medal in the 2002 Winter Olympics.

Career Highlights

1980—Michelle is born on July 7, 1980, in Torrance, California.

1985—Michelle begins skating lessons.

1987—Seven-year-old Michelle wins her first skating event.

1990—Michelle and Karen move to the Ice Castle International Training Center; Frank Carroll becomes their coach.

1992—Eleven-year-old Michelle begins skating at the senior level.

1993—Michelle wins her first major senior title at the Olympic Festival.

1994—Michelle is chosen as an alternate for the U.S. Olympic figure skating team.

1996—Michelle wins both the U.S. and world championship titles.

1997—Michelle publishes her autobiography, *Heart of a Champion.*

1998—Michelle becomes the U.S. national champion with a record number of eight 6.0 scores; she also wins the silver medal at the Winter Olympics.

2001—Michelle becomes a five-time U.S. national champion and a four-time world champion.

Words to Know

choreographer (kor-ee-OG-ruh-fur)—a person who chooses the music and arranges the jumps and moves in a skating program

competition (kom-puh-TISH-uhn)—a contest between two or more people

professional (pruh-FESH-uh-nuhl)—an athlete who is paid to participate in a sport

scholarship (SKOL-ur-ship)—a grant of money that helps a student pay for college or lessons

tutor (TOO-tur)—a teacher who gives lessons to just one student or a small group of students

To Learn More

Gatto, Kimberly. *Michelle Kwan: Champion on Ice.* Minneapolis: Lerner, 1998.

Kwan, Michelle, as told to Laura James. *Michelle Kwan, Heart of a Champion: an Autobiography.* New York: Scholastic, 1997.

Paprocki, Sherry. *Michelle Kwan.* Women Who Win. Philadelphia: Chelsea House Publishers, 2000.

Shaughnessy, Linda. *Michelle Kwan: Skating Like the Wind.* Figure Skaters. Parsippany, N.J.: Crestwood House, 1998.

Useful Addresses

Canadian Figure Skating Association
1600 James Naismith Drive
Suite 403
Gloucester, ON K1B 1C1
Canada

International Skating Union
Chemin de Primerose 2
CH 1007
Lausanne, Switzerland

U.S. Figure Skating Association
20 First Street
Colorado Springs, CO 80906

Internet Sites

ESPN.com—Michelle Kwan
http://espn.go.com/skating/s/kwanbio.html

International Skating Union (ISU)
http://www.isu.org

Skate Canada
http://www.cfsa.ca

U.S. Figure Skating Online
http://www.usfsa.org

Index